Giant Poems

Whose toes are as heavy as Venus and Mars?
What instructions would you give to a giant?
How many doughnuts can a giant eat? Find
the answers in this colourful collection of poems.

Look out for more fun Poetry Paintbox titles from Oxford.

Horse Poems	*Giant Poems*	*Water Poems*
Egg Poems	*Twins Poems*	*Minibeast Poems*
Fox Poems	*Wizard Poems*	*Weather Poems*
Sea Poems	*Space Poems*	*School Poems*
Dragon Poems	*Monkey Poems*	*Transport Poems*
Seed Poems	*Castle Poems*	*Family Poems*
Snow Poems	*Star Poems*	*Home Poems*
Sports Poems	*Pirate Poems*	*Green Poems*
Ghost Poems	*Monster Poems*	*Emergency Poems*
Mouse Poems	*Night Poems*	*Dinosaur Poems*

ISBN 0-19-916593-9

9 780199 165933

Giant Poems

Compiled by John Foster

OXFORD

Oxford University Press, Great Clarendon Street, Oxford
OX2 6DP

Oxford   New York
Athens   Auckland   Bangkok   Bogota   Bombay
Buenos Aires   Calcutta   Cape Town   Dar es Salaam
Delhi   Florence   Hong Kong   Istanbul   Karachi
Kuala Lumpur   Madras   Madrid   Melbourne
Mexico City   Nairobi   Paris   Singapore
Taipei   Tokyo   Toronto

and associated companies in
Berlin   Ibadan

Oxford is a trade mark of Oxford University Press

©Oxford University Press 1993
Published 1993
Reprinted 1996
ISBN 0 19 916593 9
Printed in Hong Kong

A CIP catalogue record for this book is available from the British
Library.

Acknowledgements
The Editor and Publisher wish to thank the following who have
kindly given permission for the use of copyright materials:

Sue Cowling for 'Fast food giant' ©1991 Sue Cowling; Eric Finney
for 'All giants' ©1991 Eric Finney; John Foster for 'Giant Griff'
©1991 John Foster; Jean Kenward for 'Ogre' ©1991 Jean Kenward;
Judith Nicholls for 'Giant tale' ©1991 Judith Nicholls; Irene
Rawnsley for 'The giant visitor' ©1991 Irene Rawnsley; John Rice
and John Foster for 'Instructions for Giants' ©1991 John Rice and
John Foster; Charles Thomson for 'Everything's giant' ©1991
Charles Thomson.

Although every effort has been made to contact the owners of
copyright material, a few have been impossible to trace, but if they
contact the Publisher correct acknowledgement will be made in
future editions.

Illustrations by
Paul Dowling, Korky Paul, Jane Gedye, Anita Jeram,
Graham Round, Dominic Mansell, Jo Burroughes.

Instructions for Giants

Please do not step on the climbing-frame
Or drink up the swimming pools.
Try not to tread on the teachers
But please flatten all the schools.

Please do not block out the sunshine.
Please do not lean on the trees.
Please push all the rain clouds away,
But please, oh please, do not sneeze!

Please duck your head when jets fly by.
Please sew up the ozone layer.
Please mind where you're putting your great big feet
Please do not tread on that chair!

John Rice and John Foster

2

4

Giant Tale

He was . . .

As wide as an oak tree,
tall as a willow;
his snore was the thunder,
a mountain his pillow.

Each step brought an earthquake,
each breath blew a gale;
one laugh moved an ocean,
each tear filled a pail.

His mouth was a crater,
with snakes for a tongue;
his eyes were the size
of the earth and the sun.

One toe was as heavy
as Venus and Mars;
his forehead was Saturn,
his hair shone with stars.

Judith Nicholls

5

Ogre

Down by the railway cutting
where the blackberries belong
they say there lives an ogre
twenty metres long.

He sleeps between the irons
that mark the broken track,
with worms and snails and foxgloves
and a girder by his back.

6

Thomas was picking berries.
He put them in a jar,
when a voice as loud as thunder
roared 'Who do you think YOU are?'

Tom ran like a greyhound
with fear inside his head!
'That's certainly an ogre
who beats up boys for bread!'

7

He turned, turned at the corner,
safely reached his door. . . .
His Mum said 'What's the hurry?
What are you running for?'

Thomas, he tried to tell her. . . .
Thomas, he tried and tried,
but he couldn't say more than 'ogre' –
the words got stuck inside.

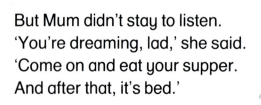

But Mum didn't stay to listen.
'You're dreaming, lad,' she said.
'Come on and eat your supper.
And after that, it's bed.'

Thomas tossed in his blanket.
He never closed an eye
until the last star faded
and morning broke the sky.

The early papers published
in letters white and black:
FOUND, A GIANT OGRE
DOWN BY THE RAILWAY TRACK!

Jean Kenward

9

Everything's giant

Everything's giant
when you're an ant.
There's a howling gale
when a dog starts to pant.

You push a boulder
(it's really a pea).
There's a buzzing plane
(it's just a bee).

Every human
is two miles high
(they cause an earthquake
when they walk by).

A blade of grass
is a mighty tree.
A puddle appears
to be the sea.

No one cares
when you puff and pant.
Everything's giant
when you're an ant.

Charles Thomson

10

All giants

'I am a giant,' said the ant.
His friends laughed one and all.
'You're crazy,' murmured butterfly,
And the bee said, 'Ant, you're small.'

'It all depends,' ant stoutly said,
'On who's compared with me.
I repeat: I am a giant –
To this microbe on my knee.'

After a little thought his friends
Said, 'Ant, that's true.
It's as you say: it all depends.
So we're all giants too!'

Eric Finney

The Giant Visitor

Great big foot came
crashing through the ceiling,
stood heel to toe
on the settee;
great big stocking,
torn about the ankle,
great big leg,
a hairy knee.

Great big voice
came booming down the chimney;
'Yoo hoo!
Is anybody there?
It's four o'clock,
I'm hungry,
so empty all your cupboards!
Cook a great big meal;

I WANT MY TEA!'

Irene Rawnsley

13

Fast Food Giant

Fast food for my giant, please,
Double-treble fries,
A fourteen-pounder in a bun,
A dozen hot fruit pies.

Fifty chicken nuggets, please.
How long will they take?
I'd better have a bucketful
Of mega-thick milk shake.

'Just a bag of doughnuts, please,
And a Monster Mac,'
He'll say with his gigantic grin –
'Delicious! When's lunch, Jack?'

Sue Cowling

14

TRY OUR DEL
CHEESEBUR

15

Giant Griff

Giant Griff
Sits on the cliff
With his legs dangling over the side.

The children stand
In a queue on the sand
To use his big toe as a slide.

John Foster

16